Keeping Unusual Pets

CHIPMUNKS

Belinda Ogle

Heinemann Library

www.heinemann.co.uk/library

To order:
☎ Phone 44 (0) 1865 888066
🖹 Send a fax to 44 (0) 1865 314091
💻 Visit the Heinemann Bookshop at www.heinemann.co.uk/library to browse our catalogue and order online.

First published in Great Britain by Heinemann Library, Halley Court, Jordan Hill, Oxford OX2 8EJ, part of Harcourt Education.
Heinemann is a registered trademark of Harcourt Education Ltd.

© Harcourt Education Ltd 2004
First published in paperback in 2005
The moral right of the proprietor has been asserted.

Editorial: Nancy Dickmann and Tanvi Rai
Design: Ron Kamen and Celia Floyd
Picture Research: Rebecca Sodergren
Production: Séverine Ribierre

Originated by Dot Gradations
Printed and bound in China by
WKT Company Limited

ISBN 0 431 12414 0 (hardback)
08 07 06 05 04
10 9 8 7 6 5 4 3 2 1

ISBN 0 431 12419 1 (paperback)
09 08 07 06 05
10 9 8 7 6 5 4 3 2 1

British Library Cataloguing in Publication Data

Ogle, Belinda
  Chipmunks - (Keeping Unusual Pets)
  636.9'364

A full catalogue record for this book is available from the British Library.

Acknowledgements

The Publishers would like to thank the following for permission to reproduce photographs:

FLPA/Minden pictures: p. 5 (top); Getty Images/Taxi: p. 25 (bottom); James Hawkins Photography: pp. 5 (bottom), 8, 10 (top), 10 (bottom), 11, 12, 14, 15 (bottom), 16, 17, 18 (top), 18 (bottom)19, 20, 21, 22, 23 (top), 23 (bottom), 25 (top), 26, 27 (bottom), 28, 29, 30, 31 (top), 31 (bottom), 32 (top), 32 (bottom), 33, 34, 35, 36 (top), 36 (bottom), 37, 38 (bottom), 39 (top), 39 (bottom), 40, 41, 44, 45 (top), 45 (bottom); MAria Joannou: p. 43 (top); NHPA/Joe Blossom: p. 4; Oxford Scientific Films/Breck P Kent/AA: pp. 9, 13; Oxford Scientific Films/Conrad Wothe/SAL: p. 6 (top); Oxford Scientific Films/E. R. Degginger/AA: p. 15 (top); Oxford Scientific Films/John Mitchell: p. 7 (top); Oxford Scientific Films/Michael Fogden: p. 6 (bottom); RSPCA Photolibrary/E A Janes: p. 42; Trevor Clifford: p. 38 (top); Tudor Photography: pp. 27 (top), 24, 43 (bottom).

Cover photograph of a chipmunk, reproduced with permission of Getty Images/Photodisc.

The Publishers would like to thank Alison's Animals, Kidlington; Witney Pet Centre, Witney; Dave Fowler and the Cotswold Wildlife Park for their assistance in the preparation of this book.

Every effort has been made to contact copyright holders of any material reproduced in this book. Any omissions will be rectified in subsequent printings if notice is given to the Publishers.

Disclaimer

Contents

Any words appearing in the text in bold, **like this**, are explained in the Glossary.

What is a chipmunk?

If you are reading this book then probably either you or someone that you know is thinking about owning a chipmunk. Not only are you considering a great pet, but you have also made a very sensible start by trying to find out as much as you can about chipmunks before you make your final decision. Far too many people buy new pets without knowing how to look after them, which only ends up making both the owner and the new pet very unhappy.

Chipmunks search for their food in trees and make **burrows** into the ground to live in.

The basics

Chipmunks are small **rodents**, which means that they come from the same family as hamsters, mice and rats. Their bodies are about 8–16 cm long with a bushy, squirrel-like tail of about 6–14 cm. Chipmunks are generally quite healthy pets and if you look after them well, and provide them with a good healthy diet, they can live for around 10 years.

Colours and markings

The most recognizable feature of a chipmunk is the stripes running down its back. Chipmunks can come in a wide variety of colours and colour combinations, although there are two main types that you will see. One is 'Agouti', which is a red/brown/grey colour with black or very dark stripes. It is the most common colour. The other is 'Dilute' which is a white/cream colour with light brown stripes.

A chipmunk is an alert, fast-moving animal who spends much of its time searching for food.

A stripey storey

There are many stories about how chipmunks got their stripes. One tells of a chipmunk that was running away from a bear who was trying to catch it and eat it. The chipmunk managed to get away just in time but the claws of the bear just touched its back and left the marks that we see today.

Stripes help chipmunks blend into the background and protect them from possible predators.

5

Where do they come from?

Chipmunks in the wild live in North America, Asia and some parts of Europe, but it is the European chipmunk, normally called the 'Siberian', that is most commonly kept as a pet.

This Siberian chipmunk is a forest animal. Its needle-sharp claws make it an excellent climber so it can look for food in trees and bushes.

This 'Least chipmunk' is one of the smallest chipmunks. It is found in more diverse **habitats** than any other chipmunk.

What's in a name?

The name 'chipmunk' is thought to come from the American Indian word 'chetaman', which means 'head first', as this is the way chipmunks climb down from trees.

Cheek pouches

Like hamsters, chipmunks have large pouches in their cheeks for carrying food. They use these to store food if they are in a hurry or if it's not safe to stop and eat it on the spot. They take their food back to a safer place to eat later.

When a chipmunk's cheek pouches are full they can be almost as large as its entire head!

Pets are a big responsibility

As with any animal, once you take on the responsibility of owning a pet, you are completely responsible for its care and its behaviour, so you need to decide if you really can provide all the care that your new pet needs.

Need to know

- It is your responsibility to make sure that your pet is healthy and well cared for. Always take your pet to the vet if it is ill or injured.
- Children are not allowed to buy any pets themselves, so you should have an adult with you when you go to buy your chipmunk.

Chipmunks in the wild

It is a good idea to find out how an animal lives in the wild, to help you understand the best way to look after it as a pet.

Where do they live?

In the wild chipmunks make their nests in **burrows** in the ground or suitable holes in a tree. They put dried leaves and grass in their nests to keep them warm. Sometimes they have more than one nest and will use the spare one for storing food.

To prepare food for storage chipmunks hold the fruit or seeds in their paws and use their incisors to remove the seeds from their pods.

Who do they live with?

Chipmunks can live alone or in pairs of one male and one female. They may also live in **colonies**, but these are spread over a large area so that they do not need to fight for the best nesting places and food. This is important to know for keeping pet chipmunks, as having two males or two females can often result in a fight.

Do they like it hot or cold?

Chipmunks come from countries with a **temperate** climate, which means that they have both cold and warm weather. Chipmunks prefer warm sunny days and normally stay in their nests if it is very cold or rainy.

A nice long sleep

If it gets too cold, as it does in some of their natural **habitats**, chipmunks will **hibernate**. This means that they go into a very deep sleep that can last for several months. Before they go into hibernation they will eat lots of food to build up fat that will help keep them warm while they are asleep, and to make sure they don't need to keep waking up to eat.

This hibernating chipmunk is curled up into a ball to keep warm. Pet chipmunks will probably not hibernate, but they may sleep for a week or two if the weather is particularly bad.

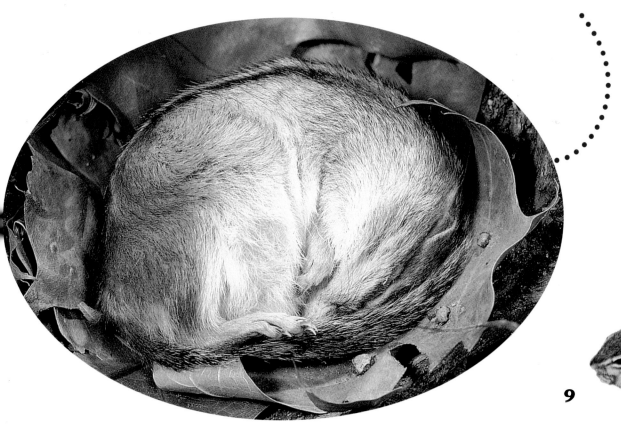

Is a chipmunk for you?

It is important to make sure that a chipmunk is the best pet for you, otherwise you will get bored and neither you nor your new pet will be happy. You need to decide if a chipmunk would suit your way of life and daily routine, and would provide you with all the things that you want from a pet.

Although they look cute and furry, chipmunks don't enjoy being picked up and stroked much.

Are they cuddly pets?

Chipmunks are very adventurous animals. They are great fun to watch, as they love exploring.

If you want a pet that you can hold and play with, then a hamster, mouse or rat would probably be more suitable for you than a chipmunk. They are not cuddly pets and can even give a nasty bite if they are not happy. However, chipmunks are great fun to watch. They are **diurnal**, and very active. They love to run, climb and dig.

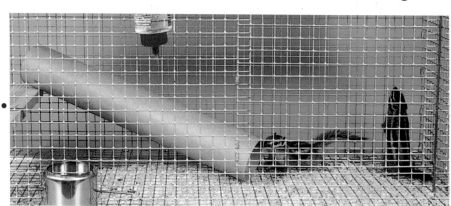

Can I tame my chipmunk?

Chipmunks are not easy pets to **tame**, so do not be upset if your pet never becomes as friendly as you would like. However, if you spend plenty of time with your chipmunk, and you get one that is quite young, there is more chance that you will be able to tame it. Some chipmunks can become tame enough to eat out of your hand, or even to sit on your shoulder. Basically they don't like to be held or feel trapped, so if you remember this and spend enough time with them they can become very friendly.

If you are patient and tempt your chipmunk with food in your hand, over time it will start recognizing you and will look forward to accepting tasty treats from you.

How much time does it take?

Any animal is a big commitment and you need to make sure that you will be able to give it all the care and attention that it needs.

A single chipmunk will need to be given fresh food and water each day. They usually go to the toilet in the same place in their cage so this spot should be cleared out each day as well. The amount of time all this takes will vary depending on how many chipmunks you have, and what sort and size of cage you keep them in.

Lots of space

Chipmunks need a lot of space. They can live indoors in a large cage, if that is the only option, but it is far better to let them have even more space in an outdoor cage.

Feeding your chipmunk doesn't take very long, but it's important that you do it every day.

Think about it

A chipmunk will take at least 15 minutes a day to look after, and that's just for its basic care. Can you commit to at least that amount of time every single day? Your chipmunk may live for 10 years or more – will you be able to look after it for this length of time?

This chipmunk is completely absorbed in preparing its dinner. It holds the nuts in its paws and cracks them open using its front teeth.

Do chipmunks need any special care?

You need to find out if there is a good vet locally who will be able to look after your chipmunk if it becomes sick. Some vets will not have much experience of chipmunks, so you may have to find a **specialist** vet who could be expensive.

Holidays

You also need to think about who will look after your pet if you go on holiday. A chipmunk is not as easy to leave as some pets, because it needs more specialist care. You will need to find someone you trust to come to your house every day and look after your chipmunk, since it is not good to disrupt chipmunks by moving them.

Breeding chipmunks

You may be thinking about breeding from your pet, but if this is the first time you have ever kept a chipmunk then you should get used to just one at first. If, however, you do want to breed, you should speak to someone who has done this before and get some good professional advice because this is a very specialized subject.

Chipmunks can be a bit naughty if you let them run around the house! They can knock things over and make a mess.

Chipmunk good points:

- They are very active and are great fun to watch.
- They are awake when you are awake.
- They are quite cheap to feed and to look after in comparison to cats and dogs.
- They are usually quite healthy and don't normally get ill.
- They are reasonably easy to look after once you get into a good routine.

Chipmunk not-so-good points:

- They are not cuddly pets.
- They can give a nasty bite.
- You will need to find someone to look after them when you go away.
- They need quite a big cage to live in which can be expensive to buy or difficult to make.
- You need quite a lot of room to keep them.
- You may need a specialist vet which could cost a lot of money.

To make a cage interesting for your chipmunk you need to install lots of branches, swings and perches.

Chipmunks have sharp teeth for gnawing and chewing. They can bite if angry or frightened, just like a dog or cat.

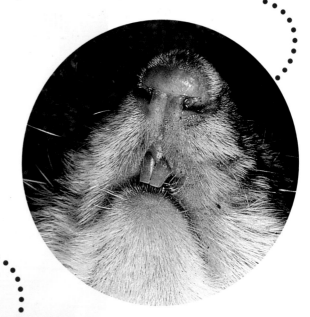

Choosing a chipmunk

Once you decide that a chipmunk is the pet for you, you need to think about what sort of chipmunk to chose.

Male or female?

If you are getting just one chipmunk it really doesn't matter whether it is a male or female. If you are getting two they should be a female and a male, since single sex pairs will fight. Obviously if you get a male and a female pair they are likely to have babies, so just keep one chipmunk if you are not ready for this. Two females and one male can be kept together, as can larger **colonies**, but this is best left to more experienced chipmunk keepers.

You should get the pet shop owner or breeder to help you identify the male and female ones as the differences in appearance are not immediately obvious.

What age?

Getting a chipmunk as young as possible is best if you want to **tame** it. A chipmunk aged 8-16 weeks is ideal. At this age it will be young enough to think of you as its 'new mum' and so it should be quite happy to come to you for food and attention, which will help if you want to tame it.

Top tip

Do not get a chipmunk any younger than 8 weeks as it will be too young to leave its mother.

Is it healthy?

It is important to get a healthy chipmunk, so there are a few things you should look out for when you choose your new pet. Make sure the chipmunk's eyes are bright and not weeping. Its fur should be shiny and it should have a bushy tail. Try and get one that is lively and **inquisitive**, as this should make it easier to tame.

Look for bright eyes and a bushy tail when you're choosing your chipmunk!

Breeder or pet shop?

It is best to get a chipmunk from a breeder rather than a pet shop. **Hand-reared** chipmunks will be a lot easier to tame. A breeder will also have lots of experience of looking after chipmunks and will be able to give you extra advice.

If possible try to see the parents of the young chipmunk you are going to buy, as this will give you an idea of how your chipmunk will grow up. A healthy tame adult is likely to produce better young. Also, watch how the chipmunk acts when the breeder tries to catch it for you. If it allows the breeder to handle it but looks **alert** and active, this is a good chipmunk to buy. If it runs away and hides or even bites the breeder it may be better to choose another one.

Get lots of advice from the breeder about chipmunk care. Don't hesitate to ask questions.

If there are lots of chipmunks in the cage you will be able to choose the one that seems the most friendly and healthy.

Be a smart shopper

If you don't know any breeders and have to get your chipmunk from a pet shop there are a few things that you can look out for to tell if it is a good shop or not. Make sure that:

- The cages are clean and that there is no bad smell.
- The chipmunks have a lot of space and are not all squashed into one small cage.
- All the animals in the shop are bright and alert, and are not hiding in the corners of the cages looking sad.
- The animals do not have runny eyes or noses, and are not covered in droppings.
- The animals have neat and clean fur and don't look as if they have been fighting.

Ask the pet shop owner about the chipmunks. If it is a good pet shop the owner should be able to give you lots of useful advice about looking after your new pet.

Make sure you look all around the cage to check it is clean and that there is fresh food and water for the chipmunks.

What do I need?

It is important to make sure that you have a good cage to keep your chipmunk in, as well as toys, bedding and food, before you buy your new pet.

Inside or outside?

You need to decide whether to keep your chipmunk inside or outside. This depends on whether you have a garden and what space you have available in it.

Indoor cages are great, since you won't need to go outside to look after your pet when it is cold or raining. Chipmunks may also become **tame** more easily if they have people moving about them all day and are kept as part of the family.

If you get an indoor cage it should be tall and airy. There should be plenty of space for your chipmunk to wander about.

The more space chipmunks have, the happier and healthier they will be.

However, the main rule for choosing or building your chipmunk cage is 'the bigger the better'. An outside cage can normally be much larger than an inside one. So unless you have the space inside to build a huge cage, it is probably best to keep your chipmunk outside.

Top tips

- If your chipmunk is going to be kept outside, the cage will need a covered area where it can hide from the wind and rain.
- Metal roofs should never be used as they can heat up in the sun and make your chipmunk too hot. They are also very noisy when it rains, which could scare your pet.

Getting a cage

The smallest cage should be 125 cm long by 95 cm wide and 125 cm tall, with at least one or two sides made of a solid material. You can buy ready-made cages, normally sold for chinchillas, that are quite suitable for chipmunks. However, the best cages are those that you make yourself, as they can be made to fit exactly into the space that you have available and to suit your requirements exactly. If you want to get into the cage to clean it out or to tame your pet, you should make sure that it is tall enough for you to stand up in easily.

It is important to make sure that the cage is completely escape-proof, since chipmunks are very good at getting through holes that you don't even know are there!

Making a new cage will let you have it exactly the way you want, but it is best to find someone who is good at making pet cages, so that it is secure.

Any wire meshing used should not have gaps between the bars that are more than 1 cm wide, as your new pet can escape through this. There is a type of wire mesh called 'weldmesh' or 'Twiweld' which is particularly good for chipmunk cages.

Getting a lock for the cage is very important, especially for an outside cage.

Check that the mesh you choose is completely safe for your pet.

Top tips

There are no real rules about how to make a cage for your chipmunk. You can make whatever sort of cage you like as long as it is:

- made of materials that are not harmful to your pet
- secure so that the chipmunk won't escape
- as big as possible and suits your own needs.

23

Nesting boxes

You will need a **nesting box** for each chipmunk that you have, so that they can feel safe at night or when it gets cold. You could buy nesting boxes that are sold for parrots and lovebirds, or you could make your own.

A nesting box like this one should be filled with hay, dried leaves or even shredded paper – although hay and dried leaves are better as this is what chipmunks would use in the wild.

In the wild, chipmunks live in **burrows** in the ground, so, as this is not possible in your cage, you could put two nesting boxes in for each chipmunk, one nearer the ground and one higher up. Whichever one they don't choose to use as a nest they can use to store food in.

Some chipmunks like to burrow, especially in outdoor cages, so make sure that the bottom of the cage is made of concrete or a similar material, otherwise your pet may soon dig its way out.

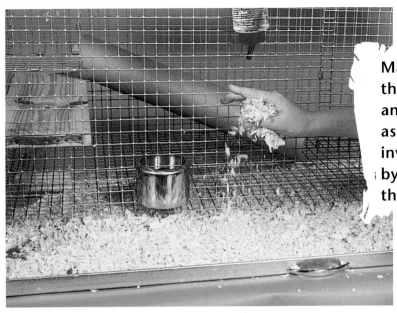

Make sure you line the base with only animal-safe materials as some chipmunks investigate things by putting them in their mouths!

Top tips

- For an indoor cage it is a good idea to have a wire mesh base to the cage, with a removable litter tray below it, as this will make cleaning it out a lot easier.
- You then need to fill the cage with things to make your chipmunk feel more at home. On top of the base you can add a thick layer of **peat** or large 'animal-safe' wood chips. This will give them something to dig in and bury bits of food.

Chipmunks like to have hiding places in the cage. In the wild, they live in burrows in the ground that are hidden by leaves and stones.

Things to climb on

Adding branches and hollow logs will give your chipmunk something to climb on, but you must make sure that they are from trees that are not harmful to your pet. Apple or pear trees are good as long as they haven't been sprayed with **pesticides**. Old cardboard tubes from kitchen rolls are a favourite with chipmunks who have fun hiding in them.

Safety first

It is always best to wash (with pet-safe cleaners) and dry any logs or branches before you put them in the cage just to be on the safe side. If you don't know whether it is safe, don't use it.

Chipmunks often chew on the wood of the branches you set up in the cage so you have to be careful that they are not poisonous.

The more you can add to the cage to make it fun and interesting for your chipmunk, the better. You can be creative when you're making a home for your chipmunk. Chipmunks love to climb and play, so they will be particularly happy if you make them a cage with lots of different levels.

Food and water bowls

You should try and get food and water bowls that are solid and heavy so that they can't be easily tipped over or chewed. Sealed water bottles that hang upside down on the side of the cage are a particularly good idea since it means that you don't have to keep clearing food or wood chips out of the water bowl. They will also reduce the chance of your chipmunk escaping because you do not need to open the door to refill them.

If you use sealed water bottles in the cage make sure they are see-through so that you can tell if the water needs re-filling.

Make sure that the food and water bowls don't have any sharp edges that could hurt your pet.

Caring for your chipmunk

Chipmunks need to be fed at least once a day, or two small meals if possible. They only eat about 30 grams of food a day, and feeding them any more will go to waste.

Feeding

In the wild chipmunks eat a very wide variety of foods, including grains like corn, oats and wheat. They also eat sunflower seeds, fruit, berries, and some protein. Ready-made food mix for chipmunks can be bought from most pet shops. These are usually very good and can make up a big part of your chipmunk's diet.

Ready-made food mix for chipmunks contains all the cereals, seeds, protein and necessary vitamins that your pet will need to stay healthy.

You should also offer your chipmunk a variety of fresh fruit. Avoid citrus fruits like oranges and lemons, as chipmunks prefer fruit such as grapes and apples. For the **protein** part of their diet, a raw egg mixed up on a heavy plate once every month is normally fine. You could also occasionally provide a few mealworms, available from most good pet shops.

Top tip

Chipmunks enjoy sunflower seeds and nuts, but you should only give these occasionally as treats because they are very fattening.

Bugs for breakfast

Chipmunks that are kept outside will normally catch the odd moth or two and eat those as well.

Fresh water should be given to your chipmunk very day. Any water that is left for longer than a day will become **stagnant** and taste bad, and could even make your pet ill.

Another thing to give your chipmunk is a **cuttlebone**. These are an excellent source of **calcium**, which your chipmunk will need to keep its bones and teeth healthy. They are also very hard so your chipmunk will chew on it, which will help stop its teeth from getting too long. Giving your chipmunk nuts in the shell will also help to keep its teeth in good condition.

Have a good look at what's available in the shop so that you can give your pet the ideal mixture of food.

Fishy food

A cuttlebone is the skeleton of a cuttlefish, which is similar to a squid. They are flat, white and look like plates. Cuttlebones are also often put in bird cages.

Cleaning the cage

Other than feeding, your main job when caring for your chipmunk is to make sure that its cage is always clean. Some things need to be done at certain times to ensure this.

Top tips

- Each week the bottom of the cage should be completely cleaned out and replaced. This will take around 15–30 minutes depending on the size of the cage.
- Every two weeks, all the toys and climbing branches should be removed and cleaned. Most good pet shops sell **disinfectants** especially for this. Never use ordinary household products; they are not made for cleaning pet cages and they can be poisonous.
- Every 2–3 months the whole cage (except the **nesting boxes**) should be completely emptied and cleaned. This could take several hours depending on the size of the cage.
- Twice a year the nesting boxes need to be washed out and dried, but never between September and March. During these months your chipmunk will have been hard at work gathering and storing food for their **hibernation**, and you shouldn't disturb this.

Keeping the cage clean will help to keep your chipmunk healthy and free of disease.

Getting into a routine

It is a good idea to get into a routine that suits you. If you are rushed and tired in the morning you won't have much time to spend with your pet. In this case you should get your chipmunk used to just being given a quick bit of food. When you get home in the evening and have more time to spend with your pet, you can give it its main feed, clean out its cage and play with it. It will soon get used to this routine and will be ready waiting for you to come home and spend some time with it.

Change the water in the bottle every day. If the water from your tap at home is good enough for you to drink then it is good enough for your pet!

Once your chipmunk is tame it will usually welcome a quick snack from you through the mesh.

31

Looking for signs of illness and injury

Chipmunks are not normally ill, but occasionally they may get the odd cold or small cut. It is a good idea to watch how your pet normally looks and behaves so that you are easily able to easily notice if it starts behaving differently or showing signs of illness or injury. If you think that your chipmunk may be unwell or injured it is best to get a good vet to take a look at it.

A butterfly net is the best way to catch a chipmunk without the risk of squashing it or scaring it too much.

An **alert**, keen-eyed chipmunk may look healthy, but you should also watch its behaviour for any signs of illness or injury.

Escaped chipmunks

You will need to learn how to catch your chipmunk in case it escapes or needs to be taken to the vet. The best way to catch a non-**tame** chipmunk indoors is to use a small butterfly net.

If a chipmunk escapes from its cage in the garden, catching it may not be so easy, even if it is tame. However, it may return to its cage by itself when it gets dark and it needs the safety of its own nesting box. You should therefore allow a suitable way in to the cage, for the chipmunk to return.

Need to know

Two or more **escapees** will unfortunately be unlikely to return. If they settle into their new home in the wild and have babies, you could get into a lot of trouble. It is **illegal** to release chipmunks into the wild, so it is a good idea to make sure that chipmunks kept in the garden can't escape at all.

If your chipmunk escapes indoors you can try to catch it by tempting it with tasty treats like peanuts or pieces of fruit.

Making friends

Chipmunks can be a lot of fun. If you have just one chipmunk it will be easier to **tame**, but it also means that you will need to spend more time with it because it will get bored on its own. Some chipmunks, however, will never become tame no matter how much time and effort you put into them.

Taking food from your hand

Once your chipmunk has settled in you can start to teach it to take food from your hand. First, drop a peanut or bit of fruit through the bars of the cage. Sit very still and talk gently to the chipmunk. Your chipmunk will notice the treat and will eventually come to pick it up when it sees you are only watching. Do this a few times until the chipmunk seems to be waiting for you to drop the treat into its cage. Next, hold the treat very still, just inside the cage. The chipmunk should come and take the food from you.

Be gentle and patient with your pet when you get close to it. This will make it learn to trust you more and feel safe coming close to you in the future.

Once you and your chipmunk are happy with this, you can try holding your whole hand inside the cage with some food on it. If you sit very still, after a while your chipmunk may come and sit on your hand to eat the food. This may take a lot of time and patience. Be very careful to make sure that it doesn't escape if you are sitting with the door open.

Handle with care!

Make sure never to try and grab your chipmunk. They need to feel totally free and not trapped in any way. If they do feel trapped they may bite, so always let them come to you when they are ready, rather than reaching for them.

Playing games

You could play 'hide and seek' with your chipmunk, using a favourite treat like a nut or piece of fruit. Try hiding these in the cage, such as in a hollow log behind a branch. You could even bury a treat in the bottom of the cage.

Once you've hidden food in various clever places in the cage, you can sit back and enjoy watching how long it takes your chipmunk to find them.

Getting adventurous!

You can create your own adventure playground for your chipmunk including ropes, tunnels, hammocks and even a slide. Be as creative as you can! As long as all the parts that you use are safe and there is no way for your pet to hurt itself, both you and your chipmunk can have a lot of fun.

Make sure you set up the cage before you put your chipmunk in or it might get scared.

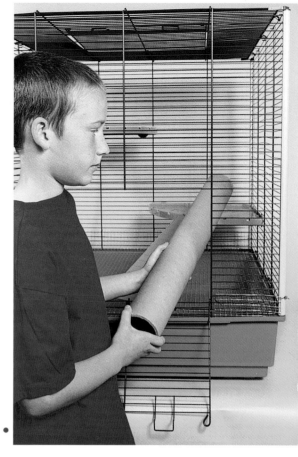

Place several treats in a long, winding trail around the cage with something extra special at the end, and see if your chipmunk will follow the trail. Once your chipmunk has learnt how to do this, you can add some obstacles, like ropes and tunnels, and teach it to follow an obstacle course.

Swings and ladders work very well in chipmunk cages as they love to explore them and run up and down.

Once your chipmunk is very tame you may be able to let it out in a 'safe room' in the house. It is especially important to make sure that all other household pets are well out of the way.

Always make sure that all windows are closed and that there are no escape holes.

Top tips

- You should never let your chipmunk out of its cage into a room unless it is very tame, otherwise you will not be able to catch it to return it to its cage.
- There are many things in the home that could be dangerous for a chipmunk, so you must also make sure that it is completely safe to let your pet out.

Some health problems

Chipmunks do not normally get very ill, but occasionally they may get a disease or injury that will need a vet to look at it. Most of the problems your chipmunk could have are likely to be caused by giving them the wrong food or the wrong materials in their cage, and these can be easily solved. However, if the **symptoms** do not clear up in a few days, or if the animal seems to be getting worse or is in pain, you should get a vet to have a look at it as soon as possible.

Diarrhoea

If you notice that your chipmunk's droppings are very runny, this means it has **diarrhoea**. This is usually nothing to worry about and probably means it has eaten a bit too much fresh fruit and vegetables. Make sure that you feed a larger amount of cereals in its diet until its droppings look normal again, and try not to feed it as much fresh fruit and vegetables in the future.

If you are ill yourself ask somebody else at home to look after your chipmunk for a few days.

This is what healthy chipmunk droppings should look like. They are firm and fairly dry.

If you keep a record of your chipmunk's health it will be easier to notice if anything changes, and you can give proper detailed information to the vet.

Constipation

This is the opposite of diarrhoea, when your chipmunk's droppings are very hard or it seems as if your chipmunk is unable to go to the toilet at all. This is also not usually a problem and is often caused by your chipmunk not eating enough fresh fruit and vegetables. Alternatively, it could be because you have given it 'cotton-wool' style bedding which it may have eaten, causing it to get all blocked up. Giving it larger amounts of fresh fruit and vegetables and changing its bedding to straw should sort out this problem.

Eye problems

Eye problems can occur if you use very fine wood shavings to line the bottom of the cage. The small pieces of wood can get into your chipmunks eyes and cause them to become infected and 'weepy'. If you remove any materials from the cage that could be causing this and replace them with more suitable things, the problem should clear up on its own.

Very fine wood shavings (top) can give your pet health problems. Always use larger, animal-safe wood shavings (bottom) to put in the cage.

39

Cuts and small wounds

Occasionally you may notice that your chipmunk has a small cut or wound. Normally these are caused by something sharp inside the cage, like part of the wire meshing or a bit of a log or branch. Make sure that all sharp edges have been smoothed off. If the injury is not too bad, it should heal by itself in a few days but if the injury looks bad or does not heal, you should get a vet to look at it.

Alternatively, if you have more than one chipmunk in the cage, the injury could be caused by a fight. In such a case you may need to separate the chipmunks to stop them from hurting each other again.

Make sure that the mesh of the cage is not wide enough for a chipmunk to put its head through as this can cause serious injury.

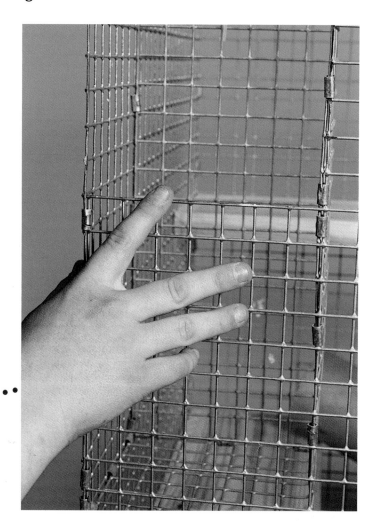

Overgrown teeth

One common problem in chipmunks is overgrown **incisors**. This can be prevented by giving your pet a **cuttlebone** to chew on and by giving them nuts in their shells, which should help to wear the teeth down a bit. If they do become overgrown you should take your chipmunk to the vet as soon as possible. Your pet may have trouble eating if its teeth get too long and it may not be getting enough food.

Old age

Although not an illness, old age may bring with it a few signs that your pet is not quite itself. They will start to look a bit tired and even start to look a bit grey. Unfortunately there is nothing that you or your vet can do to stop your pet from growing older! As long as it still seems to be enjoying its life, just be gentle with it and let nature take its course.

If you are unsure about what is wrong or what you need to do to help a sick or injured chipmunk you should take it to the vet.

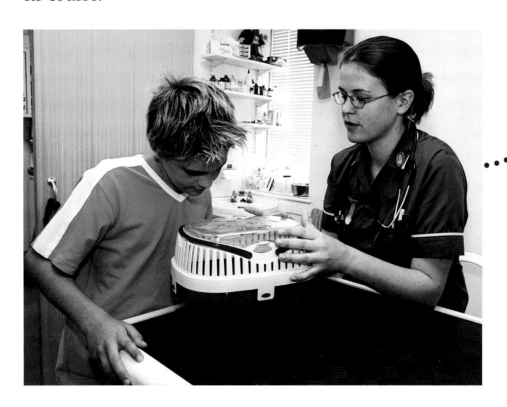

When a chipmunk dies

Sadly the time will come when your pet will die. This is a very natural thing and there is nothing that you can do to stop it from happening some day. It doesn't matter how well you look after your pet, one day it will be time for it to go. Sometimes this will happen without warning and you may discover your pet has passed away during the night. Other times you may be aware that your pet is sick or old and the vet may tell you that it will die very soon.

When chipmunks get old they put on weight and become sluggish. Their fur goes slightly grey too.

Putting to sleep

Sometimes you and your vet may feel that a sick or very old chipmunk is no longer enjoying its life and that the kindest thing to do for it would be to 'put it to sleep'. The vet will simply give your pet an **injection**, which won't hurt it. The chipmunk will fall into a deep sleep and its heart will stop. It won't feel any pain and it will be over very quickly. This is a very difficult decision to make but it is also a very brave one, and one that shows you are trying to do what is best for your pet.

Feeling sad

When something that we love dies, it is a very difficult and sad time. It is important to understand that your pet didn't suffer in any way and that it died peacefully after a happy life. Death is just one of those things that happens and it is not your fault in any way.

It is normal for both children and adults to cry when a loved pet dies or when we think about a pet that has died. After a while the sadness will pass and you can just remember the good times that you had with your pet.

It can help to have a special burial place for your pet. You can decorate your pet's grave with flowers and pebbles.

Feeling sad only means that you had a very good friendship with your pet, which is something to be proud of.

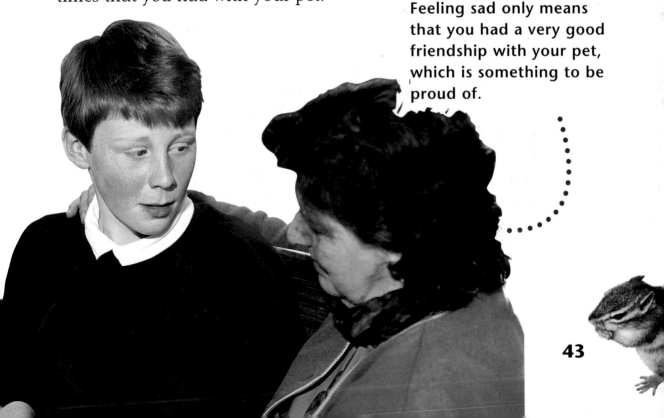

43

Keeping a record

Just like any friend or member of your family, your pet should have a place in your photo album, or even an album all of its own. This will be fun to create, and once your pet has died it will give you something to remember it by.

It is a nice idea to make notes about your chipmunk, like when you first brought it home and how you **tamed** it. You could keep a diary of all the things that you did with your pet and the progress it made as you tamed it and taught it new tricks.

Take photos of your chipmunk with different members of your family and all your friends that come round, and create a 'hall of fame' with all the people that your chipmunk has played with. You can then make up funny captions to go with the pictures or make a comic-style book about your chipmunk.

You can have great fun taking lots of pictures of your chipmunk doing all the things that it enjoys.

There may be a chipmunk club nearby that you could join and meet other people that have chipmunks. Have a look on the internet or ask your vet if there are any local clubs that you could join.

Why not keep a scrapbook full of cut-outs from magazines and articles that you find about chipmunks? You can really be creative, decorating it with lots of pictures and including some of your own drawings. You could even write your own book about keeping and caring for chipmunks!

Remember to write dates against the pictures so that you know when they were taken.

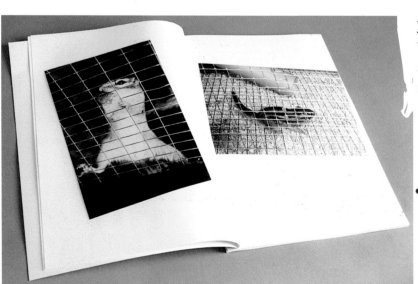

You can take your scrapbook to school to show off your beautiful pet!

45

Glossary

alert   aware of what is going on around it, lively

burrow   a hole dug out in the ground as a place to live, hide or store food

calcium   substance found in some foods that helps to keep bones healthy

cheek pouches   stretchy skin around the mouth that makes it possible to store lots of food there for short periods

colony   a group of creatures that live together

constipation   having trouble going to the toilet

cuttlebone   dried out, white flat bone of a squid-like creature

diarrhoea   runny droppings

disinfectant   special medicated cleaning liquid

diurnal   happening during the day

escapees   the ones that have got away, escaped

habitat   place where an animal or plants lives or grows

hand-reared   brought up by humans, not in the wild

hibernate   go into a long, deep sleep in a warm place to cope with cold weather

illegal   against the law

incisors   front teeth

injection   medicine given using a needle

inquisitive   curious

nesting box   warm and cosy wooden box for chipmunks to rest and sleep in

peat   natural plant material used to line a cage

pesticides   chemicals used to kill insects and other pests that damage crops and livestock

protein   substance found in some food that helps creatures to grow

rodent   furry animal with strong front teeth for gnawing

stagnant   something that has been sitting around for ages; not clean and fresh

specialist   an expert who is specially good at something

symptoms   signs that indicate something specific

tame   used to being with people

temperate   not too hot or cold

Useful addresses

The Royal Society for the Prevention of Cruelty to Animals (RSPCA) has regional offices, clinics and animal centres all over the UK. They will be able to give you advice on how to care for your chipmunk and what to do if it becomes sick. To locate the one closest to you visit their website.

RSPCA (London headquarters)
20 Station Road
South Norwood
London SE25 5AJ
http://www.rspca.org.uk

More books to read

Your First Chipmunk, James Wilkie, (Kingdom Books, 1998)

Pet Owner's Guide to the Chipmunk, Chris Henwood, (Ringpress Books, 1998)

Guide to Owning Chipmunks and Similar Species, (TFH Publications, 1998)

Helpful websites

http://www.chipmunks.info – Good information about what they eat, where they live and more.

http://animaldiversity.ummz.umich.edu/accounts/tamias/t._sibiricus $narrative.html– Provides a detailed account of Siberian chipmunks' natural history, care and behaviour.

http://www.petz.co.uk/information/chipmunkinfo.html – Gives a gist of chipmunk behaviour and care as well as a list of books to read.

http://www.rodentrefuge.co.uk – Gives general information about rodents.

Index